First World War
and Army of Occupation
War Diary
France, Belgium and Germany

41 DIVISION
Headquarters, Branches and Services
Royal Army Veterinary Corps
Assistant Director Veterinary Services
1 March 1918 - 30 September 1919

WO95/2624/6

The Naval & Military Press Ltd
www.nmarchive.com
Published in association with The National Archives

Published by

The Naval & Military Press Ltd

Unit 10 Ridgewood Industrial Park,

Uckfield, East Sussex,

TN22 5QE England

Tel: +44 (0) 1825 749494

www.naval-military-press.com

www.nmarchive.com

This diary has been reprinted in facsimile from the original. Any imperfections are inevitably reproduced and the quality may fall short of modern type and cartographic standards.

© **Crown Copyright**
Images reproduced by permission of The National Archives, London, England, 2015.

Contents

Document type	Place/Title	Date From	Date To
Heading	WO95/2624/6		
War Diary	Camposampiero	01/03/1918	02/03/1918
War Diary	Mont be Court	03/03/1918	07/03/1918
War Diary	Leucheux	08/03/1918	21/03/1918
War Diary	Baizieux	22/03/1918	22/03/1918
War Diary	Bihucourt	23/03/1918	23/03/1918
War Diary	Greyellers	24/03/1918	25/03/1918
War Diary	Souastre	31/03/1918	31/03/1918
War Diary	Bailleulval	28/03/1918	28/03/1918
War Diary	St Amand	29/03/1918	04/04/1918
War Diary	Steenvoorde	05/04/1918	10/04/1918
War Diary	Hyde Camp Area Brandhoek	11/04/1918	27/04/1918
War Diary	Ten Elms	28/04/1918	29/04/1918
War Diary	La Lovie	30/04/1918	03/06/1918
War Diary	Nieurlet	04/06/1918	07/06/1918
War Diary	Eperlecques	08/06/1918	26/06/1918
War Diary	Oudezeele	27/06/1918	02/07/1918
War Diary	Abeele	03/07/1918	07/07/1918
War Diary	K.24 C.2.3	08/07/1918	31/07/1918
War Diary	Sheet 27 K. 24. C.2.3.	01/08/1918	14/08/1918
War Diary	K. 24. C.2.3.	15/08/1918	29/08/1918
War Diary	Wizernes	30/08/1918	03/09/1918
War Diary	L 14 a 2.0	04/09/1918	29/09/1918
War Diary	Mersey Cross G 23.C.7.5	30/09/1918	17/10/1918
War Diary	Dadizeele	18/10/1918	22/10/1918
War Diary	Bisseghem	23/10/1918	31/10/1918
War Diary	T'Hooge	01/11/1918	02/11/1918
War Diary	St Louis	03/11/1918	07/11/1918
War Diary	Vichte	08/11/1918	10/11/1918
War Diary	Kerkhem	12/11/1918	12/11/1918
War Diary	Grammont	27/11/1918	29/11/1918
War Diary	Kerkhem	12/11/1918	14/11/1918
War Diary	Nederbrackel	15/11/1918	18/11/1918
War Diary	Santbergen	19/11/1918	21/11/1918
War Diary	Grammont	22/11/1918	10/12/1918
War Diary	Engien	12/12/1918	12/12/1918
War Diary	Hal	13/12/1918	13/12/1918
War Diary	Braine	14/12/1918	14/12/1918
War Diary	L'Allved Marbais	17/12/1918	17/12/1918
War Diary	Mazy	18/12/1918	18/12/1918
War Diary	Waret La Chaussee	19/12/1918	19/12/1918
War Diary	Vinalmont	20/12/1918	11/01/1919
War Diary	Marienburg	12/01/1919	31/05/1919
War Diary	Cologne	02/06/1919	28/06/1919
War Diary	Marienburg	02/09/1919	30/09/1919

WAR DIARY or INTELLIGENCE SUMMARY

Army Form C. 2118.

DADVS 472

Vol 23

Place	Date	Hour	Summary of Events and Information	Remarks and references to Appendices
CAMPOSAMPIERO	1.3.18		O.S. Lat.— Headquarters entrained at CAMPOSAMPIERO for FRANCE.	
	2.3.18		Mobile Section entrained.	
MONT de COURT	3.3.18		Headquarters detrained at MONT de COURT and marched to COUTUREHE. Office at HUMBERCOURT	
	4.3.18		M.K.S. detrained and marched to LEUCHEUX	
	5.3.18		Visited O.C. polyectr at COUTUREHE, M.K.S. LEUCHEUX	
LEUCHEUX	6.3.18		Headquarters & Office moved to LEUCHEUX and M.K.S. to LES ANNETTES FARM COUTUREHE	
	7.3.18		Visited 122, 123, 124 Brigade areas	
	8.3.18		Visited 123, 125, 124 Brigade areas	
	10.3.18		Visited M.K.S. and 4 depôts	
	11.3.18		Visited D.A.C.	
	12.3.18		Visited 190th Brigade R.F.A. On arrival	
	13.3.18		Visited A, B, C Batteries 189 Brigade R.F.A.	
			190 Brigade R.F.A. T.M. & A.S.C.	

WAR DIARY
or
INTELLIGENCE SUMMARY.
(Erase heading not required.)

Army Form C. 2118.

Place	Date	Hour	Summary of Events and Information	Remarks and references to Appendices
NEUCHELLES	14.3.18		Inspection of Returns by Lucas	
			XIII Corps H. FREVENT to Effect reliefs & organisation	
	15.3.18		Opened up Gunner at FREVENT. Visited 235 Sy	
			R.E. at OPPY	
	16.3.18		300 mph. conference at IV Corps. Inference at	
			D.H.Q. Visits to R.E. Army & 13th H.Q. Pg. 1	
			& Log Mechanic Sec. Coy	
	17.3.18		Visit to M.V.S.	
	18.3.18		Visit to 18 y old 19 m R. alo R.F.A.	
	19.3.18		Visit to M.V.S. + N.Z. + A.S.C.	
	20.3.18		M.V.S. moved to LOUVEN COURT	
	21.3.18		Louven to BAIZIEUX	
MAIZIEUX	22.3.18		D.H.Q. moved to BIHUCOURT	
			M.V.S. + G.J. to ADHINSVELLE	
BIHUCOURT	23.3.18		to PREVELLERS	

Army Form C. 2118.

WAR DIARY
or
INTELLIGENCE SUMMARY.
(Erase heading not required.)

Instructions regarding War Diaries and Intelligence Summaries are contained in F. S. Regs., Part II. and the Staff Manual respectively. Title pages will be prepared in manuscript.

Place	Date	Hour	Summary of Events and Information	Remarks and references to Appendices
SAVELLERS	24.3.18	3.p	M.V.S. Arrived to PUISEUX. Advance post for M.V.S. opened at work hour REW ABLAINZEVELLE	
	25.3.18		M.V.S. & Dress'n to ACHIET LE PETIT	
		10 p	M.V.S. back to SOUASTRE	
SOUASTRE	26.3.18		M.V.S. Truck'd to ST AMAND	
			Evacuation of wounded LAHERLERE Rubber	
	28.3.18		A bus brought to BAILLEULVAL	
			M.V.S. transferred to ST AMAND	
ST AMAND	26.3.18		M.V.S. Arrived to ST AMAND	
			M.V.S. Truck'd to AUTHIE Bicycles	
	30.3.18		Visited 187, 128, 124, 2F.A. and Machine Gun Battalions	
	31.3.18		Visited 187 and 190 Brigades R.F.A. Inspected 176 Remounts at SOUASTRE	

Wl. B. Giles Major
D.A.D.V.S.

WAR DIARY
or
INTELLIGENCE SUMMARY.

Army Form C. 2118.

Place	Date	Hour	Summary of Events and Information	Remarks and references to Appendices
St AMAND	1.4.18		I.O. Recc^e Visited 187 Bryg^{de} OR. R.F.A	
	2.4.18		Visited 187 and 190th Bryg^es R.F.A.	
	3.4.18		Head Quarters moved to PETIT-HOUVEN and entrained for BELGIUM.	
	4.4.18		Head Quarters detrained at PESELHOEK & moved to STEENVOORDE	
STEENVOORDE	5.4.18		M.V.S detrained PESELHOEK & moved to HAEZEWINDE	
			Visited No 3 & 4 Sys F.S.C & 139 Fd Ambulance	
	6.4.18		Divisional conference at VIII Corps.	
	7.4.18		Visited M.V.S	
			M.V.S. moved to 5 a.8.8. Sheet 27.	
			Visited 133 O.F.C. Bryg^{de} & 19th Middlesex Pioneers	
	9.4.18		Visited site for M.V.S	
	10.4.18		Office work referred to G4 H.5. Sheet 28	
			M.V.S. moved to 3.5.5.H.H.	
			Visited 19th Middlesex Pioneers & Trench Mortar Battn	

WAR DIARY
or
INTELLIGENCE SUMMARY.
(Erase heading not required.)

Army Form C. 2118.

2nd Q Leek

Place	Date	Hour	Summary of Events and Information	Remarks and references to Appendices
HYDE CAMP ALL BRAND HOEK	11.4.18		Visited 126 Coy. Brigade and 3 Coys R.E.	
	12.4.18		Visited 14 Bde R/C R.F.A.	
	13.4.18		Attended Conference VIII Corps and No 1 Coy A.S.C. 29th Division	
	14.4.18		Visited Y Bde R.H.A. 19 Middlesex Fusrs & Machine Gun Battalion	
	15.4.18		Visited D.A.C. 29th Division	
	16.4.18		Visited 15 Bde R.H.A.	
	17.4.18		Visited M.V.S.	
	18.4.18		Visited 132 & 1230 Infantry Brigades	
	20.4.18		Attended Conference a2 - 11 Corps & Inspected A.S.C.	
	21.4.18		Visited 124th Infantry Brigade & 9 Field Quartermaster	
	22.4.18		Visited 17 Bgde R.F.A.	
	23.4.18		Visited D.H.Q. 29 Division	

WAR DIARY
or
INTELLIGENCE SUMMARY.
(Erase heading not required.)

Army Form C. 2118.

Place	Date	Hour	Summary of Events and Information	Remarks and references to Appendices
HYDE CAMP AREA BRANDHOEK		3rd of Feb.		
	24.4.18		Visited M.V.S.	
	25.4.18		Visited 17" Brigade R.F.A. Conference Veterinary Officers	
	27.4.18		Attended Conference at 11 Corps Office Dover St	
TEN ELMS			Ten Elms Remount	
	28.4.18		Inspection 1M Remounts. Visited D.A.C. 29th Div with anti steril Quantus	
	29.4.18		Visited 139 Field Ambulance. Office Move to La Lovie Chateau	
LA LOVIE	30.4.18		Visited Machine Gun Battalion, 122 & 124 Inf Brigades	
			Date of Formation of usyn Feb 13. 1915	
			O. Mule Vet. Sectn Oct 30. 1915	
			Date of Proceeding Overseas from U.K. April 29. 1916	
			Hyn O.C. Kys	
			D.A.D.V.S.	

WAR DIARY
or
INTELLIGENCE SUMMARY.
(Erase heading not required.)

Army Form C. 2118.

DADVS 41 D

Vol 25

Date	Hour	Summary of Events and Information	Remarks and references to Appendices
LADVS			
1.5.18		Visited M.V.S.	
2.5.18		Conference of Veterinary Officers. Visited A.S.C.	
3.5.18		Attended Conference 11 Corps. A.D.V.S. H.Q.	
4.5.18		Visited 122 & 124 Inf. Bgdes & Machine	
		Gun B. attached. Conference D.M.Q.	
5.5.18		Visited 139 Field Ambulance & 9th D.A.C.	
6.5.18		Visited 15th Bde R.F.A.	
7.5.18		Visited 138 & 140 Field Ambulances	
8.5.18		Visited 19 Middlesex Pioneers & 3 Coys R.E. and	
		S.A.A.	
9.5.18		Inspection of 52 M.V.S. by A.D.V.S. 11 Corps	
		& visit to 139 Field Ambulance	
10.5.18		Visited M.V.S.	
11.5.18		Conference of 11 Corps	
12.5.18		Visited 122 Inf. Brigade & Machine Gun Battalion	
13.5.18		Inspection of A.S.C.	

WAR DIARY
or
INTELLIGENCE SUMMARY
(Erase heading not required.)

Army Form C. 2118.

Place	Date	Hour	Summary of Events and Information	Remarks and references to Appendices
LA LOVIE	14.5.18		Visited 122 & 12th Army Brigades	
	15.5.18		Visited D.A.C. 20 D.V.S. 190 Brigade R.F.A.	
	16.5.18		Conference of Veterinary Officers 78 & Bde R.F.A	
	17.5.18		Inspection of 33 Rendy[?] Bry & R.F.A	
	18.5.18		Conference of 11 Corps	
	19.5.18		Visited Machine Gun Battalion	
	20.5.18		Inspection of 41st D'n arm'd Arttery by A.D.V.S. 11 Corps	
	21.5.18		Visited 13 Field Ambulance M.V.S.	
	22.5.18		Establishes an arm'ed Veterinary Aid Post at A 23 C.S.S. Visited Artillery units	
	23.5.18		Conference of Veterinary Officers Capt. F. R. PAGE deputed to carry on from Ju 23 Veterinary Hospital	
	24.5.18		Capt A.J.S. REYNOLDS proceeded to No 2 Base Depôt Remounts HAVRE, O.Inspection of D.A.C.	

Army Form C. 2118.

WAR DIARY
or
INTELLIGENCE SUMMARY.
(Erase heading not required.)

Instructions regarding War Diaries and Intelligence Summaries are contained in F. S. Regs., Part II. and the Staff Manual respectively. Title pages will be prepared in manuscript.

Place	Date	Hour	Summary of Events and Information	Remarks and references to Appendices
LA LOVIE	25.5.16		Visited artillery of 122" Infantry Brigade	
	26.5.16		Attended conference II Corps. O. & gdn.en	
			55 Reinforcements at D.A.C.	
	27.5.16		Reported 138 & 140 F.W.A. & Infantries	
	28.5.16		Inspected 41, 23 C.S. Brigade 3 Companies	
			M.R.E. 19 F. Inspected Futureen	
			Inspected A190 Brigade M.V.S	
	29.5.16		Visited 123 & 124 by artillery Brigades	
	30.5.16		Conference Corps Officers	
	31.-			
	31.5.16		Inspected D.S & S # Army Accompanied by	
			A.D.V.S. II Corps. D.V 13 B Offices 107 Brigade RFA	
			B. Battery HQ Brigade RFA	
			C. Inspected 3rd Portsmouth Tanks	
			Date of Formation of H¼ Durham S.H. 13.1.915	
			52 M.V.S. Oct. 30, 1915	
			— Proceeding overseas from U.K. April 29, 1916	

C. W. T. Lyttle Major DADVS

WAR DIARY
or
INTELLIGENCE SUMMARY.
(Erase heading not required.)

Army Form C. 2118.

DADVS 41/2 Vol 26

Place	Date	Hour	Summary of Events and Information	Remarks and references to Appendices
LA LOVIE	1.6.18		Inspection of Artillery Brigades	
	2.6.18		Attended "Experience" XI Corps. I visited M.V.S.	
	3.6.18		Inspection of Artillery Brigades	
			52" M.V.S. proceeded to ZEGGERS CAPPEL	
NIEURLIET	4.6.18		D.H.Q. moved to NIEURLIET. Inspection 2.3 Fd Coys A.S.C.	
			32" M.V.S. proceeded to KINDER BEUK	
	5.6.18		Inspection 112" & 6" Brigade & M.R.S.	
	6.6.18		Inspection 72 & 91 Brigade & 139 Field Ambulance	
	7.6.18		D.H.Q. moves to EPERLECQUES	
EPERLECQUES	8.6.18		Influenza at VII Corps. Visited 13/20 & Brigade	
			138 Field Ambulance	
	9.6.18		Inspection of 32" M.R.S. by A.D.V.S. VII Corps.	
			Visited 187 Brigade R.F.A.	
	10.6.18		32" M.V.S. proceeded EPERLECQUES H33/55./2/A	
			Visited & witnessed Tanks	
	11.6.18		Visited D.A.C.	

WAR DIARY
or
INTELLIGENCE SUMMARY.
(Erase heading not required.)

Army Form C. 2118.

Place	Date	Hour	Summary of Events and Information	Remarks and references to Appendices
EPERLECQUES	12.6.18		Inspection of 190th Brigade R.F.A.	
	13.6.18		Visited 123 & 95 Bm Cdrs - N/sence of Veterinary Officers	
	14.6.18		Visited 189 Bde R.F.A.	
			Att. Lieut. J.A.V.C. reported for duty to 63 Div.	
	15.6.18		Visited 125 1/2 H O.R. & A.V. Brigade parked	
	16.6.18		Visited D.A.C.	
	17.6.18		3 Horses Board & examined Horses of Messines Rd.	
	18.6.18		Attended Board & examined horses 1/125 O.R.A.	
	19.6.18		2 TT's del Board & examined horses of 124 O.R.A Brigade	
			Assisted to 134 O.R. Brigade	
	20.6.18		Visited 189 Brigade R.F.A.	
	21.6.18		Assisted in D.A.C. Absence of Veterinary Officers	
	22.6.18		Visited Horse Lines of Artillery	
			Visited 15 1/2 & 1/4 1/5 Bdes	
	23.6.18		Visited 238, 233 R.F.A. 94/31 T/38 Field Ambulance	

WAR DIARY
or
INTELLIGENCE SUMMARY.
(Erase heading not required.)

Army Form C. 2118.

3rd Sheet

Place	Date	Hour	Summary of Events and Information	Remarks and references to Appendices
EPERLECQUES	24.6.18		Visited M.V.S.	
	25.6.18		Inspection of 15" Army Auxiliary Horse T. & Siege Coy R.E. 52nd M.V.S. proceeded to ZEGGERS CAPPEL	
	26.6.18		D.H.Q. & Office formed at WIZERNES	
OUDEZEELE	27.6.18		Visited No 11 M.A.S.C. Income & No Battalion F/9 Thunderbolt	
	28.6.18		Visited & shown Schemes & Aux Horse Transport	
	29.6.18		Visited 124 & St. andrey Brigade	
	30.6.18		Visited 123 & and army Trey ade —	

Date of formation of Division Sep 13, 1915
Do — do — 52nd M.V.S. Oct. 30, 1915
By proceeding Overseas from U.K. April 29, 1916.

Lt Col Villiers
D.A.D.V.S.

WAR DIARY or INTELLIGENCE SUMMARY

Army Form C. 2118.

DADVS 47D

Vol 27

Place	Date	Hour	Summary of Events and Information	Remarks and references to Appendices
OUDEZEELE	1.7.18		Visited M.V.S.	
	2.7.18		Feed Quarters & Office Arrgts to Aerodrome ABEELE	
ABEELE	3.7.18		Inspection of 190th Bde ammn R.F.A.	
	4.7.18		Inspection of 187 " " RFA	
	5.7.18		Visited 12A & Devanshy Brigade	
	6.7.18		Visited 132 FB & 3 Cavalry Brigades	
	7.7.18		D.H.Q & Place forward to 27/15 24 C.C.S.	
M.14.C.2.3	8.7.18		Visited 3 Cdn. R.E. T.19 Infld Sec Pioneers	
	9.7.18		Inspection Sundry Details by A.D.V.S. XIX Corps	
	10.7.18		Visited 134th Cav Bgde & Pln ale	
	11.7.18		Visited 12th Cav. Bde ale Med. Veterinary Officer	
	12.7.18		D Ward " " " " XIX Corps	
	13.7.18		Visited 133 Cavalry Brigade	
	14.7.18		Visited 124th Cavalry Brigade & 3 Cavs R.E.	
	15.7.18		Visited 190 Bde amm R.F.A.	
	16.7.18		Visited 187 Bde amm RFA	

WAR DIARY
or
INTELLIGENCE SUMMARY.
(Erase heading not required.)

Army Form C. 2118.

Place	Date	Hour	Summary of Events and Information	Remarks and references to Appendices
K24 C28	17.7.18		At Nel 3. Visit A.S.C. Advance & Veterinary Officers	
	18.7.18		Casualties reported Bombs on E/Lr 2/15th Bn 2	
			Sectors D&C 13 O.Rs Killed & 16 Mules wounded	
			2 Horses in Harness despatched 138 Field A. Amb.	
	19.7.18		Visited D.A.C. & M.V.S.	
	20.7.18		Visited Vaccine Yard Britain.	
	21.7.18		Visited M.V.S. 122 Infantry Brig.	
	22.7.18		Inspection of M. Gun Bat. & R.E. by ADVS. XIX Corps	
	23.7.18		" 122, 123 & 124 Inf. Brig. "	
	25.7.18		Remounts at DAQ Sector S.A.D. inspected.	
			Visited 187 & 190 R.F.A.	
	26.7.18		Visited M.V.S.	
	27.7.18		Inspected at Divisional Train.	
	28.7.18		Visited M.V.S.	
	29.7.18		Major C.W.B. Liked granted 14 days leave to England.	

Army Form C. 2118.

WAR DIARY
or
INTELLIGENCE SUMMARY.

(Erase heading not required.)

Sheet B.

Place	Date	Hour	Summary of Events and Information	Remarks and references to Appendices
K.24. C.2.3.	29.7.18.		Capt. J. Macdonald A.V.C. acting for D.A.D.V.S.	
	30.7.18.		Inspected 12th Infantry Brigade. Visited M.V.S. & evacuated sick. Visited 206th F.R.E.s	
	31.7.18.		Inspected 41 Divisional Signal Coy. 10th R.M. Kents & 23rd Middlesex. Visited M.V.S. & evacuated sick.	

Date of formation of 41 Division. 13.9.15.
" " 53rd M.V.S. 30.10.15.
" " 29.4.16.
Proceeded overseas.

J. Macdonald: Capt. A.V.C.
for D.A.D.V.S.

DADVS 47 Army Form C. 2118.
VOL 28

WAR DIARY
or
INTELLIGENCE SUMMARY.
(Erase heading not required.)

Sheet =

Place	Date	Hour	Summary of Events and Information	Remarks and references to Appendices
Sheet 27				
K.24.c.23.	1.8.18.		Visited M.V.S. & evacuated sick. Conference of Veterinary Officers.	
	2.8.18.		Visited 124 Infantry Brig: & M.V.S.	
	3.8.18.		Visited ADVS XIX Corps, 138 Field Ambulance, 26 Roy. Fusiliers, 10 R.W.Surreys & M.V.S.	
	4.8.18.		Inspected 187 Bry: R.F.A. & 10 R.W.Kents & 11th R.W.Surreys	
	5.8.18		Visited 23rd Middlesex, Divisional Signals & M.V.S.	
	6.8.18.		Conference of officers at A.D.V.S. Office XIX Corps. Visited M.V.S.	
	7.8.18.		Visited 124 Inf: Brigade & M.V.S., 138 Field Ambulance.	
	8.8.18.		Visited Divisional Signals, 10 R.W.Kents, & 23rd Middlesex & M.V.S. Conference of officers.	
	9.8.18.		Visited 124 Infantry Brigade & M.V.S., & 41 Divisional Signals.	
	10.8.18.		Inspected 190 R.F.A. & 298th R.F.a.	
	11.8.18.		Visited 10th R.W.Kents, 23rd Middlesex & M.V.S. Visited M.V.S. 41 Divisional Signals TT05702 A/F/Sme Cpl Nathan E. reported here.	
	12.8.18.		Visited 41 Div: Signals, 124 Inf: Brig: & M.V.S.	
	13.8.18.		Visited M.V.S.	
	14.8.18.		Visited 41 Div. Signals, 10 R.W.Kents & 23rd Middlesex & M.V.S. Major C.W.B. Sikes returned from leave.	

WAR DIARY
or
INTELLIGENCE SUMMARY.
(Erase heading not required.)

Army Form C. 2118.

Place	Date	Hour	Summary of Events and Information	Remarks and references to Appendices
M 24 c 2.3.	15.8.16		O feet 2	
	16.8.16		Visited 123 & 134 O Vantry Brigades	
	17.8.16		O spected 190 Brigade R.F.A.	
	18.8.16		Conference at X Corps Hestony A.S.C. T.M.V.S.	
			Preliminary Inspection plan for Infantry Station	
			Visited 123 & Infantry Regiments	
	19.8.16		Conference D.A.C.	
	20.8.16		O spected 187 Brigade R.F.A	
	21.8.16		O spected 138 F.A. & Division	
			Inspected C of E Ranks 8A & C R.E.	
	22.8.16		O spected from 330 to 331 Brigades R.F.A.	
	23.8.16		Visited 123 & 124 Infantry Brigades	
	26.8.16		O spected 138 F.W Ambulance	
	27.8.16		O spected 190 Brigade R.F.A.	
	28.8.16		O spected 187 Brigade R.F.A.	

WAR DIARY
or
INTELLIGENCE SUMMARY.
(Erase heading not required.)

Army Form C. 2118.

Place	Date	Hour	Summary of Events and Information	Remarks and references to Appendices
WIH C.2.3	29.8.16		Sheet 3. D.H.Q. & Officers moved to WIZERNES	
WIZERNES	30.8.16		Visited HQ of 3 Coy A.S.C.	
	31.8.16		Visited 123 Infantry Brigade	
			D.A.D.V.S. arrived. Division left WIZERNES Feb 13.1915. Made return to Sch: Oct 30 1916.	
			D.V.S. proceeding to the sums from U.K. April 29.1916	
			MB Aylmer Anzele D.A.D.V.S.	

WAR DIARY
or
INTELLIGENCE SUMMARY.
(Erase heading not required.)

Army Form C. 2118.

PADVS 47/5

Vol 30

Place	Date	Hour	Summary of Events and Information	Remarks and references to Appendices
WIZERNES	2.9.18		Rec'd 1	
			Strength 128 Bicycle Orderly	
	3.9.18		D.H.Q. 7 Officers strength 7 h 1 H A 2.2.0	
			M.K.S. Strength 13 d 3.5.	
	4.9.18		Inspection 132 Mob Bde aux 1387 & F.A.S.	
	5.9.18		Inspection of Veter. Officers Inspection of	
			Remounts	
	6.9.18		Re-inoculation taken up M.P.S.	
	7.9.18		M.K.S & met Col 5/26 & 3.19	
LHA 3.0	8.9.18		Actively taking inside entries internal I/95	
	9.9.18		Visited 16 D.A.C.	
	10.9.18		Visited 16 P Bgde R.F.A	
	11.9.18		H.J.S.O travel to Army Vrm to GIM11 M.A.S.C	
	12.9.18		A.D.V.S XIX Corps Inspected M.K.S.	
			Inspected Veterinary Officer situated 20 h.D.m	
	13.9.18		Inspected 3 Cavs Bde Cat situated 20 h.D.m	
			each unit Im in large sized Mules	

WAR DIARY
or
INTELLIGENCE SUMMARY

(Erase heading not required.)

Army Form C. 2118.

Place	Date	Hour	Summary of Events and Information	Remarks and references to Appendices
L In a 2.0	15.9.18		M.K.S. Battery to L.88.c.8.4. Verdict of 38.b.73.9 Field Ambulance	
	16.9.18		Casualties 190 Bde R.F.A.	
	19.9.18		Reconnaissance for site for Sidney Tube	
	22.9.18		Visit (with early) Brigade	
	19.9.18		Reconnaissance of trenches of 95 Bde Stables	
	20.9.18		Cooperation of Artillery	
	21.9.18		D1- XIX Corps visit M.K.S.	
	22.9.18		Reconnaissance of D.H.Q. Rendezvous	
	23.9.18		Visits to F.L.23 Trench Map 28. Rendezvous	
	24.9.18		Battery 3 Guns F.2.5	
	27.9.17		Cooperation 139 F/Ho Fires A.M. Issues	
			Day of MacLean of R. Jones. Reconnoitre to Sherpenburg R.F.A	
	26.9.18		M.K.S. B. Trench 190 Bde on R.F.A.	

Army Form C. 2118.

WAR DIARY or INTELLIGENCE SUMMARY.
(Erase heading not required.)

Place	Date	Hour	Summary of Events and Information	Remarks and references to Appendices
L.H.Q.	2.00 19.9.16		2 Regl 3	
			Reconnoitring & H batn of M.R.S. & it owned G lines	
	28.9.16		M.R.S took to G 23 d H 5. Outward dressing Station at H 13 d. H 5.	
	29.9.16		Office IDHQ moved to MERSEY CROSS G 23.C.Y.5.	
MERSEY CROSS G 23.C.Y.5	30.9.16		Ordnung dressing Statn moved to H 32 d. 9.4. Yesterday Ourwert dressing Statn to be kept in transport.	
			Don't Mortarter H.D. Mison Supt. 13.9.1916 Transfer of B2 M.F.S. to J. 30. 9. 16. Proceeding Residue from U.K. April 24 1916	

Wts O Pegg Capt
DADVS

WAR DIARY
or
INTELLIGENCE SUMMARY.
(Erase heading not required.)

Army Form C. 2118.

D.A.D.V.S.
41st DIVISION.
No. ....
Date 31/10/18

Place	Date	Hour	Summary of Events and Information	Remarks and references to Appendices
MERSEY CROSS A.D.S. G.23.c.7.5	1.10.18		Reconnoitred for Ambrose for M.V.S.	
			M.V.S. arrived H.16.c.9.0.	
			Lieut. W.E. Stebbing attached for duty	
	2.10.18		Tour of Armoured Bde/etc. W O & L.L.B.	
	3.10.18		Visited D.A.C. etc	
			Visited A.C. Elson O.C. Van In Bque & 169/Buyde R.F.A.	
	4.10.18		Visited A.D.M.S. XIX Corps	
	5.10.18		Visited 122, 124 & 5/6 by Bgades 41st 3 Bgde	
	6.10.18		A.S.C. & D.A.C. — Reconnoitring Rd. forward	
	7.10.18		Visited 187, 190 Bgds. & R.F.A.	
	8.10.18		M.V.C. 1 horse in Depot 513 O.V. Bgade	
	9.10.18		Visited 123, 124 O.L. and 18/	
	10.10.18		5 Sick & 1 horse destroyed—Ambulance & Horse also	
			D.A.C. — M.V.S.	
	11.10.18		M.V.S.	

WAR DIARY or INTELLIGENCE SUMMARY

Army Form C. 2118.

D.A.D.V.S., 41st Division

Place	Date	Hour	Summary of Events and Information	Remarks and references to Appendices
MERSEY CROSS G.23.O.Y.S.	13.10.18		Visit. T. M.V.S. 122 H 123 Q S[?] Cavalry Brigade	
	14.10.18		123rd R.E. Sqdn. D.H.Q. V[?]S.N. Cavalry Bde etc	
	15.10.18		Visited A. Echelon D.H.Q & 30 Cavalry Brigade	
	16.10.18		Visited No. 1 Coy A.S.C. & DADIZEELE	
	17.10.18		Horses Removed to DADIZEELE	
DADIZEELE	18.10.18		D.A.C. Y/122 O.N. Cavalry Brigade	
	19.10.18		Visited 190 Bde. R.F.A.	
	20.10.18		Visited 187 Bde ade. R.F.A.	
	21.10.18		M.K.S. & H.Q. & 141 F.A. 5.10	
	22.10.18		Office moved to BISSEGHEM M.K.S. moved to BISSEGHEM	
BISSEGHEM	23.10.18		Visited 122 & Cavalry Brigade 19th Middlesex Pioneers, 2/8 R.E. M.T. & O Field Ambulance	
	24.10.18		Visited M.V.S. & Cavalry Brigade	
	25.10.18		Visited R.E. T 138 Field Ambulance	

WAR DIARY
or
INTELLIGENCE SUMMARY.

(Erase heading not required.)

Army Form C. 2118.

Place	Date	Hour	Summary of Events and Information	Remarks and references to Appendices
BISSEGHEM	26.10.18		Visited 19th Bde & R.F.A.	
	27.10.18		Visited 187 Bde & R.F.A.	
	28.10.18		Visited 12 & 11 Cavalry Brigades	
	29.10.18		Visited and attended a T.H. & G.H.	
			Visited Machine Gun Battalion	
	30.10.18		Visited D.A.C. Veterinary Officers	
	31.10.18		Angels in B	
			B.W.S.D. totol 13.10.15	
			Total M.V.S. Oct. 3rd 1915	
			M.D.S. Oct. - U.K. Oct Sept.14	
			Proceeding Prisoners from U.K. Oct Sept.14	
			(sgd) A. Wilson	
			Major	
			D.A.D.V.S.	

WAR DIARY or INTELLIGENCE SUMMARY

Army Form C. 2118

Part V Vol 32

Place	Date	Hour	Summary of Events and Information	Remarks and references to Appendices
T'HOOGE	1.11.18		Visited 190th Brigade RFA.	
	2.11.18		Officer killed at St LOUIS. MKS. Arthur & N.B. 8.	
ST LOUIS	3.11.18		Visited 237 FC. & 187 Brigade RFA & 190 Brigade RFA	
	4.11.18		Visited 19th Masheen Pataur 188 Field Amber	
	5.11.18		A & D Batteries 190 Br. etc.	
			MKS Arnwl St Louis	
	6.11.18		" A 199 Brigade RFA	
			" 190 Brigade RFA	
	7.11.18		Visited front at YCHTE	
	8.11.18		" 190 Brigade RFA MKS St LOUIS	
YCHTE	9.11.18		J.F.C. 3.4.	
	10.11.18		Visited at XL wharf	
			MKS Arrived at YCHTE	
			Visited 190 Br & DAC	
KERKHEM	11.11.18		Official March to KERKHEM.	

Army Form C. 2118.

WAR DIARY
or
INTELLIGENCE SUMMARY.
(Erase heading not required.)

Instructions regarding War Diaries and Intelligence Summaries are contained in F. S. Regs., Part II. and the Staff Manual respectively. Title pages will be prepared in manuscript.

Place	Date	Hour	Summary of Events and Information	Remarks and references to Appendices
GRAMMONT	27/11/18		Ref 3	
	28/11/18		Visited 12 & 08 Yantry Bns also the 11th Army Field Brigade A.D.V.S. 10 corps inspected all A.F.A. Brigade Transport to returned to Div 8te	
	29/11/18		Visited No 2 and 3 Fd Bttlns.	
			Daily Fourders H D Wicus Feb 13 1915	
			52nd M.V.S. Oct 30, 1915	
			Proceeding Pusse for UK April 4, 1916	
			A.D.V.S. D.V.S.	

Army Form C. 2118.

WAR DIARY
or
INTELLIGENCE SUMMARY.
(Erase heading not required.)

Instructions regarding War Diaries and Intelligence Summaries are contained in F. S. Regs., Part II. and the Staff Manual respectively. Title pages will be prepared in manuscript.

Place	Date	Hour	Summary of Events and Information	Remarks and references to Appendices
			Sheet 2	
BERKHEM	12.11.18		M.V.S. Met to Q 21.6.6/19	
	13.11.18		Visit to 190 Bay Bde	
	14.11.18		9 pieces and M.V.S. A.MC to NEDERBRACKEN	
NEDERBRACKEN			R.F.A	
	15.11.18		Visit to 187 Bde R.F.A	
	16.11.18		Inspection of Remounts	
	17.11.18		Visit to 12 N.C. Infantry Bde 6.65	
	18.11.18		9 piece Arme to SANTBERGEN	
SANTBERGEN	19.11.18		M.V.S. and 30/116 B.O.	
			Visit to 187 B/ade R.F.A	
	21.11.18		9 piece Arme to GRAMMONT	
GRAMMONT	22.11.18		Visit to 113 Sy mony Bn R.F. Corps	
			Mrs C. Glenn to GRAMMONT	
	23.11.18		Visit Louise Tournament Cheese	
	24.11.18		Visit 133 1 Coy O.C. alway Binges	
	26.11.18		Visit to Machine gun Battalion	

26/m

DADV S4712 Vol 3 3

Army Form C. 2118.

WAR DIARY
or
INTELLIGENCE SUMMARY.
(Erase heading not required.)

Instructions regarding War Diaries and Intelligence Summaries are contained in F.S. Regs., Part II. and the Staff Manual respectively. Title pages will be prepared in manuscript.

Place	Date	Hour	Summary of Events and Information	Remarks and references to Appendices
GRAMMONT	1/12/18		Strength - 187 ORs and 190 Brigades R.F.A.	
	2/12/18		Statistical D.A.C.	
	3/12/18		Proceeded to X Corps of A.D.V.S.	
	4/12/18		Inspection of Veterinary Officers	
	5/12/18		Visited D.A.C. 19 X Trips wagons & Princess YMVS	
	6/12/18		" " B.A.C. & M.V.S.	
	7/12/18		Visited No. 1. Cav. Train	
	8/12/18		Visited D.A.C.	
ENGHIEN	12/12/18		Office moved to ENGHIEN	
HAL	13/12/18		Office moved to HAL	
BRAINE	14/12/18		Office & Baine L'Arrue arrived	
LILOES MARBAIS	15/12/18		Office moved to MARBAIS	
MAZY	16/12/18		Office moved to MAZY	
WARET La CHAUSSEE	17/12/18		Office moved to WARET La' CHAUSSEE	
VINALMONT	18/12/18		Office moved to VINALMONT	
	19/12/18		M.V.S. arrived to HUY	

WAR DIARY
or
INTELLIGENCE SUMMARY.

Army Form C. 2118.

Place	Date	Hour	Summary of Events and Information	Remarks and references to Appendices
MALMONT				

WAR DIARY
or
INTELLIGENCE SUMMARY.
(Erase heading not required.)

Army Form C. 2118.

D.A.D.V.S.,
41st Division.

Place	Date	Hour	Summary of Events and Information	Remarks and references to Appendices
VINALMONT	1.2.19		Visited 123 & 124 Bys — Bugle	
	2.1.19		Visited 190 Bde & R.F.A.	
	3.1.19		Brady examining horses R.E. 138 Feb Amb	
	4.1.19		Visited 124 Siege Bty & A.S.C.	
			" " " H. Ambulance & Bde Ammn Column	
	5.1.19		Visited M.V.S.	
	6.1.19		Brady Infect. Hosp — Iarnwells D.H. &	
	7.1.19		Infection of nurses D.W. & 3rd Army	
			M.V.S. Brady sent to HUY	
	8.1.19		Visited Town Mayor A.B.D. Brunsh 11 Bde	
	9.1.19		Advanced A.B.y. 183 the D 191 Bde	
	10.1.19		March to MARIENBURG	
MARIENBURG	11.1.19		Settling in at MARIENBURG	
	13.1.19		M.V.S. at work at MARIENBURG 13 Bde H.Q.	
	15.1.19		Board Gas-filled Wag Hog R.R., R.E. Machine Gun	
			Brade + A.S.C.	

WAR DIARY or INTELLIGENCE SUMMARY

Army Form C. 2118.

Place	Date	Hour	Summary of Events and Information	Remarks and references to Appendices
MARIENBURG	16.1.19		Bonus Inspection 13/9 Field Ambulance	
			2/3 M.G.R.E.	
	17.1.19		Inspection H.Q. 13 Bde, H.Q. 123 Infantry Bde, 2/3 M/kent Regt	
	18.1.19		Baths by No 2, 3 Inf Bdes, D.A.C.	
	19.1.19		Conference of Staff Officers	
	20.1.19		Inspection of 190 Bde, R.F.A. HQ 122 Bde 138 FW Ambulance, No 3 M. A.S.C.	
	21.1.19		Inspection of H.Q. 8. 189 Bde R.F.A., S.A.A. Sectn S.H.C. 2/ QRDAC	
	22.1.19		Inspection of 122, 124 O.S. Bde 18 KRR Regt, 15-17 April M.O.E. Surrey Regt	
	23.1.19		Inspection of 228 Sq R.E., 140 Field Ambulance, MT Coy A.S.C.	
	24.1.19		Inspection of No 2 M. Coy A.S.C. B/Coy Machine Gun of Middlesex Princess	

WAR DIARY
or
INTELLIGENCE SUMMARY.
(Erase heading not required.)

Army Form C. 2118.

Place	Date	Hour	Summary of Events and Information	Remarks and references to Appendices
MARIENBURG	23.1.19		Feb 3 M.K.S.	
	26.1.19		Railway movements at MARIENBURG Barracks	
	27.1.19		Class front'r 210 grenadiers & 26 R.F. Engineers	
	28.1.19		Moonlight ? B/M 74 sieme Grun Bn N. D	
			M 14 Grenr Rgt. R.F.A.	
	29.1.19		Visited 190 Bde R.F.A	
			To O.A.K. SNYDER B.A/C.	
	30.1.19		A.C.M. Marshall Bn R.R.	
			A.D.V.S. X Corps	
			R & O Cav Machine Guns Bn	
	31.1.19		Linnisch M. D'Wasm Feb 13 1915	
			232nd M.K.S. Oct 30 1915	
			D.W. Sch. Linnich April 29 1916	
			M.K.S. J.W.G. 4 J.M. BADVS	

WAR DIARY or INTELLIGENCE SUMMARY

Army Form C. 2118.

DIARY 4/1 Divr
Feb 35

Place	Date	Hour	Summary of Events and Information	Remarks and references to Appendices
MARIENBURG	2.2.19		Arrived from Capelver & Crefeld	
	3.2.19		Attended Conference at 10th R.M. Regt. Pty.	
	4.2.19		En route to F.A.	
	5.2.19		Visited 12 & 13 HBde	
			Visited A.S.C.	
	6.2.19		Conference of Veterinary Officers	
	7.2.19		Lecturing at X Corps BONN	
	8.2.19		Conference of Indust Bde's Veth Anbce	
	9.2.19		Visited RFA	
	10.2.19		Visited A.R Bty, 10 Bde RFA, M.T.	
	11.2.19		Visited 13th Fd Ambulance & No Mob Lab	
	12.2.19		Holloway Army Svc	
	13.2.19		Attended 19th Bde RFA	
	14.2.19		Attended B.M Cav's HQ	
	15.2.19		Attended 3 M Cav's R.E.	
			Holloway & Wantry Bdes	
	16.2.19		Visited 13th Wantry Bde	

WAR DIARY
or
INTELLIGENCE SUMMARY.

Army Form C. 2118.

Place	Date	Hour	Summary of Events and Information	Remarks and references to Appendices
MARIAMBURG	17/2/16		Reel 2. Visited 123 Q & Anty Bde.	
	18.2.16		Inspection 19 M'cny'rs Pioneers 237 Coy RE & A. Son M.G. Bn	
	19.2.19		Inspection 237 Coy RE 19 M'dlsex P 27 Coy M.G.B.	
	20.2.19		Inspection 2/3 Coys A.S.C. HEUMAR	
	21.2.19		Visited 100 Bde R.F.A. D.A.C.	
	22.2.19		Visited M.V.S.	
	23.2.19		Visited A.D.V.S.	
	24.3.19		Inspection 190 Bde R.F.A. D.A.C.	
	25.2.19		Inspection 184 Bde R.F.A.	
	26.2.19		Inspection 123 & Anty Bdes	
	27.3.19		Visited A.D.V.S. X M'cyrs & M.V.S.	

DeptH FINNIGAN M Dwain Sept. 13.1915
D Sgt Mrs. Bd Sq 10.15
Proceedings missing for U.K. Club 8.9.16
Luto. C Mts. LS ADVS

WAR DIARY
or
INTELLIGENCE SUMMARY.
(Erase heading not required.)

Army Form C.

Instructions regarding War Diaries and Intelligence Summaries are contained in F. S. Regs., Part II. and the Staff Manual respectively. Title pages will be prepared in manuscript.

Place	Date	Hour	Summary of Events and Information	Remarks and references to Appendices
MAGDEBURG	2/3/19		Visited 19th Middlesex Pioneers, 228 Coy R.E. & Coy Machine Gun Battalion	
	3.3.19		Inspected 138 D.H. Field Ambulance Coy Machine Gun Battalion & 23rd Middlesex R.I.	
	4.3.19		Visited M.V.S.	
	5.3.19		Visited 190 Bde. R.F.A.	
	6.3.19		Visited M.V.S.	
	7.3.19		Attended Conference + Corps	
	8.3.19		Conference Bde OC's Bde.	
	10.3.19		Visited 198 Bde R.F.A.	
	11.3.19		Attended Execution Court Enquire	
	12.3.19		Administration Conference	
	13.3.19		Attended internment Camp	
	14.3.19		Inspected D.S.? No.1 Coy A.S.C.	
	15.3.19		Visited M.V.S.	

Army Form C. 2118.

WAR DIARY
or
INTELLIGENCE SUMMARY.
(Erase heading not required.)

Instructions regarding War Diaries and Intelligence Summaries are contained in F. S. Regs., Part II. and the Staff Manual respectively. Title pages will be prepared in manuscript.

Place	Date	Hour	Summary of Events and Information	Remarks and references to Appendices
MARIENBURG	1/3/19		2 fld. 2 Inspection H.S.C.	
	19.3.19		Inspection of 139 Field Ambulance. Major C.M.B. Sikes A.R.V.S. left on leave to U.K.	
	20.3.19		Inspection & animals at 2nd Army Animal Concentration Camp. Inspected A Coy. M. Div: Train. Visited M.V.S.	
	21.3.19		Inspected 52nd Batt. Notts & Derby Regiment. Visited M.V.S. & evacuated sick.	
	22.3.19		Visited Animal Concentration Camp, & M.V.S.	
	23.3.19		do. do. do.	
	24.3.19		do. do. do. Inspected H Coy. Div: Train.	
	25.3.19		do. do. do.	
	26.3.19		Visited "A" Coy. Machine Gun Batt: 3 & 4 Coy Div: Train, & M.V.S.	
	27.3.19		Visited Animal Concentration Camp, & M.V.S. & Northern Div: Animal Reception Camp	
	28.3.19		Visited M.V.S.	
	29.3.19		do.	
	30.3.19		Visited M.V.S. & London Div: Animal Concentration Camp.	
	31.3.19		Visited M.V.S. Capt. Dickinson R.A.V.C. reported for duty.	

J.J. Macdonald
Capt.

Army Form C. 2118.

WAR DIARY
or
INTELLIGENCE SUMMARY.
(Erase heading not required.)

Instructions regarding War Diaries and Intelligence Summaries are contained in F. S. Regs., Part II. and the Staff Manual respectively. Title pages will be prepared in manuscript.

Place	Date	Hour	Summary of Events and Information	Remarks and references to Appendices
MARIENBURG	1.4.19.		Visited H.Q. 190.R.F.A., Loi Annual Reception Camp & M.V.S. Capt. R.B. Crichton. R.A.V.C. & Capt. P. Hodgins R.A.V.C. reported for duty.	
	2.4.19.		Visited M.V.S. & D.A.R.C.	
	3.4.19.		do do do	
	4.4.19.		Visited M.V.S.	
	5.4.19.		Capt. F.R. Page R.A.V.C. & Lieut. W.F. Stibbling R.A.V.C. proceeded to Concentration Camps for demobilization. Capt. P.W. Walker R.A.V.C. reported for duty. Visited M.V.S.	
	6.4.19.		Visited M.V.S.	
	7.4.19.		Major C.W.B. Sykes R.A.V.C. returned from leave.	
	8.4.19.		Res Jou M.V.S. & Wounded Animal Reception Camps	
	9.4.19.		Inspection of 1 & 2 Worker Bureau & Conference of Officers on any Services	
	10.4.19.		Handed over to Major S.F. Macdonald R.A.V.C. and departed for demobilization	

Army Form C. 2118.

WAR DIARY
or
INTELLIGENCE SUMMARY.
(Erase heading not required.)

Sheet 7

Instructions regarding War Diaries and Intelligence Summaries are contained in F. S. Regs., Part II. and the Staff Manual respectively. Title pages will be prepared in manuscript.

Place	Date	Hour	Summary of Events and Information	Remarks and references to Appendices
MARIENBURG	11.4.19		Visited M.V.S.	
	12.4.19		Attended court-martial on Pte. Chrystal, A. of 52 M.V.S. Accused was acquitted.	
	13.4.19		Visited M.V.S. Major C.N.B. Like S.A.V.C. reported to No 7 Concentration Camp, Cologne, for demobilization	
	14.4.19		Visited M.V.S. & L.A.R.C.	
	15.4.19		Visited M.V.S.	
	16.4.19		Attended Conference at A.D.V.S. Ti Corps. Visited M.V.S. Conference of Veterinary officers. Visited M.V.S.	
	17.4.19			
	18.4.19		Capt. T. Hodglin granted leave 19.4.19 to 3.5.19. took over M.V.S.	
	19.4.19		Visited M.V.S.	
	20.4.19		Major E. Hearne reported for duty as D.A.D.V.S	Ent.
	21.4.19.		Visited M.V.S. at Minakow London Vet Animal Reception Camp	Ent.
	22.4.19		Attend conference at A.D.V.S. 6th Corps	Ent.
	23.4.19		Inspected L.A.R. Camp	Ent.

WAR DIARY
or
INTELLIGENCE SUMMARY.
(Erase heading not required.)

Army Form C. 2118.

Sheet III

Place	Date	Hour	Summary of Events and Information	Remarks and references to Appendices
MARIENBURG	24.4.19		Inspected 117 Bde. Riga	S+
	25.4.19		" 3rd London Infantry Brigade	S+
	26.4.19		Visited M.E.S. - Divisional H.Q. and Signals	S+
	27.4.19		Visited M.E.S.	S+
	28.4.19		Inspection 1st London Inf. Bde. - C Coy M.G. Battn - 233 Field Coy R.E.	S+

Strenue Major Park

OCOVS London Division

Army Form C. 2118.

WAR DIARY
or
INTELLIGENCE SUMMARY.
(Erase heading not required.)

Sheet 1.

Instructions regarding War Diaries and Intelligence Summaries are contained in F. S. Regs., Part II. and the Staff Manual respectively. Title pages will be prepared in manuscript.

Place	Date	Hour	Summary of Events and Information	Remarks and references to Appendices
MARIENBURG	1.5.19		Visited 3 Batts. 190 Bde. R.F.A. and D.A.C.	Sgd.
"	2.5.19		Div. H.Q. + Signal Coy and 52 M.T.S.	Sgd.
"	3.5.19		London Div. Animal Reception Camps.	Sgd.
"	5.5.19		Div. Signal Coy and Div. H.Q. – attended G.O.C's conference. Arranged	Sgd.
"	6.5.19		No.1 Coy Div. Train. Inspected M.F.S. and Div. A.R.C. with A.D.V.S.	Sgd.
Do—	7.5.19		M.F.S. + D.A.R.C.	Sgd.
"	8.5.19		2, 3 + 4 Coys. Div. Train	Sgd.
"	9.5.19		Attended conference at A.D.V.S II Corps	Sgd.
"	10.5.19		Visited 2nd London Inf. Bde. – Duty at D.D.V.S's Office	Sgd.
"	11.5.19		Duty at D.D.V.S's Office	Sgd.
"	12.5.19		Inspected 3 Batts. 189 Bde. + 3 Batts. 190 Bde. R.F.A. with A.D.V.S. II Corps	Sgd.
"	13.5.19		Duty at D.D.V.S's Office	Sgd.
"			Inspected 138, 139 +1140 Field Ambs. Duty at D.D.V.S's Office	Sgd.
"	14.5.19		Visited D.H.Q. + Signal Coy. —do—	Sgd.
"	15.5.19		M.F.S. —do—	Sgd.

WAR DIARY
or
INTELLIGENCE SUMMARY.
(Erase heading not required.)

Army Form C. 2118.

Sheet II

Place	Date	Hour	Summary of Events and Information	Remarks and references to Appendices
MARIENBURG	16.5.19		Duty at D.D.V.S'. Office	S.H
"	17.5.19		—do—	S.H
"	18.5.19		—do—	S.H
"	19.5.19		—do— Visited L.D.V.R.C.	S.H
"	20.5.19		—do— Visited " and M.V.S.	S.H
"	21.5.19		—do—	S.H
"	22.5.19		—do— Visited "C" Batty 190 Bde R.F.A. and 228 Field Coy R.E.'s	S.H
"	23.5.19		—do—	S.H
"	24.5.19		—do—	S.H
"	25.5.19		—do— Visited Divl HQrs & Signal Coy R.E.	S.H
"	26.5.19		—do—	S.H
"	27.5.19		—do—	S.H
"	28.5.19		—do—	S.H
"	29.5.19		—do—	S.H
"	31.5.19		Visited 1st London Inf. Bde. — 3 Coy. M.G. Batln. — and M.V.S.	S.H

K Munro. Major D.A.D.V.S.
Lon. Div.

WAR DIARY
or
INTELLIGENCE SUMMARY.
(Erase heading not required.)

Army Form C. 2118.

Sheet I

DADVS

Place	Date	Hour	Summary of Events and Information	Remarks and references to Appendices
COLOGNE	2/6/19		Visited 52 M.V.S., Divl. HQ & Signals, 9th E. Surveys	
	3/6/19		with ADVS 6th Corps, Inspected N°1 Coy A.S.C.	
	5/6/19		Conference of Veterinary Officers	
	6/6/19		Inspected Remounts for Divisions	
	7/6/19		Visited ADVS 6th Corps	
	9/6/19		Inspected 2nd London Infantry Bde & 23rd Royal Fusiliers	
	11/6/19		Visited 3 Coy of R.E., Divl. HQ & Signals	
	10/6/19		52 M.V.S.	
	11/6/19		"	
	12/6/19		Inspected M.G. Battn. & "C" Batty. 190 Bde R.F.A.	
	13/6/19		Visited Divl. HQ & Signals	
	14/6/19		19 Fusiliers, 19 Middlesex, 26 R. Fusiliers, "A" & "B" 187 Bde R.F.A., & HQ 3rd London Inf. Bde.	
	16/6/19		7 V.V.S.	
	17/6/19		London DAC and ADVS 6th Corps	
	18/6/19		DVS in forward Area	
	20/6/19		"	

Army Form C. 2118.

WAR DIARY
or
INTELLIGENCE SUMMARY.
(Erase heading not required.)

Sheet 1.

Instructions regarding War Diaries and Intelligence Summaries are contained in F. S. Regs., Part II. and the Staff Manual respectively. Title pages will be prepared in manuscript.

Place	Date	Hour	Summary of Events and Information	Remarks and references to Appendices
COLOGNE	21/6/19		Visited Forward Area	
	23/6/19		" "	
	24/6/19		Div. HQ of Signals	
	25/6/19		No 1 Coy Div. Train, Div. HQrs of Signals	
	26/6/19		Office Routine	
	27/6/19		Visited Squadron of Cavalry attached to Divn, 1 Coy RE's, 3 Coy A.S.C, Fd Ambulance, M.T.S	
	28/6/19		Office Routine	

V. Hodgins Capt.
for Major, R.A.V.C.
D.A.D.V.S. London Division

D.A.D.V.S.
41st DIVISION.
No.................
Date...............

Army Form C. 2118.

WAR DIARY
or
INTELLIGENCE SUMMARY.
(Erase heading not required.)

Instructions regarding War Diaries and Intelligence Summaries are contained in F. S. Regs., Part II. and the Staff Manual respectively. Title pages will be prepared in manuscript.

Place	Date	Hour	Summary of Events and Information	Remarks and references to Appendices
MARIENBURG	2.9.19		Inspected Nº 2, 3 & 4 Coys Divl Train	
	3		Visited 52 M/S, D.H.Q. & Signals	
	4		" C.R.A.	
	5		Inspected "A" Batty 190 Bde R.F.A.	
	6		Visited C.R.A.'s horses	
	9		Inspected 140 Field Ambulance	
	10		" A, B & D Batteries 190 Bde R.F.A.	
	11		" "A" Batty 189 Bde R.F.A.	
	12		Inspected C Batty 190 Bde R.F.A. & 1st London Inf Bde.	
	13		" HQ 2nd London Inf Bde. 2/4 Queens & 10th Queens	
	15		" London DAC.	
	17		Visited 52 M/S, D.H.Q. Signals	
	18		Inspected HQ 3rd London Inf Bde. 17th & 26th R. Fusiliers	
	19		" 11th Queens	
	22		" 17th Queens	
	23		" 19th Middx (Pioneers)	

Army Form C. 2118.

WAR DIARY
or
INTELLIGENCE SUMMARY.
(Erase heading not required.)

Instructions regarding War Diaries and Intelligence Summaries are contained in F. S. Regs., Part II. and the Staff Manual respectively. Title pages will be prepared in manuscript.

Place	Date	Hour	Summary of Events and Information	Remarks and references to Appendices
	24		Visited 52 MVS.	
	25		Conference of N.O.?	
	26		Visited MVS	
	27		" 6th Inniskilling Dragoons	
	28		" 2nd London Inf Bde	
	29		" 52 MVS & 6 Inniskilling Dragoons	
	30		"	

E W Scoby
Major RAVC
DADVS
London Div

www.ingramcontent.com/pod-product-compliance
Lightning Source LLC
Chambersburg PA
CBHW081246170426
43191CB00037B/2059